A Cup of Cold Water

Small Deeds with Eternal Significance

by
Lloyd D. Grimm, Jr.

Author of
Called to be a Pastor
Great is Thy Faithfulness
I Will Arise
Sixty-six Days, Sixty-six Books

St. Matthew 10:42

Schmul Publishing Company
NICHOLASVILLE, KENTUCKY

Cover image Copyright: <a href='https://www.123rf.com/profile_junpinzon'>junpinzon / 123RF Stock Photo</a>. Used by permission.

Published by Schmul Publishing Co.
PO Box 776
Nicholasville, KY 40340
USA

Printed in the United States of America

ISBN 10: 0-88019-607-6
ISBN 13: 978-0-88019-607-9

Visit us on the Internet at www.wesleyanbooks.com, or order direct from the publisher by calling 800-772-6657, or by writing to the above address.

Contents

DEDICATION

I lovingly dedicate this book to my beloved wife, Fern, who has given a life of service in the building of God's Kingdom; and to my son, John, in preparing this manuscript for publication; also to Schmul Publishing Company (especially Curtis and Myrna) who have done so much to encourage me in my retirement ministry of writing.

PREFACE

GOD'S WORD PLACES emphasis on the small deeds that are done by his followers because they are disciples of Christ. In the Gospel of St. Matthew 10:42 we read, "And whosoever shall give to drink unto one of these little ones a cup of cold water only in the name of a disciple, verily I say unto you, he shall in no wise lose his reward."

No doubt many genuine children of God have a tendency to feel unless they are engaged in some monumental task, nothing of importance is being accomplished. But, God's Word contradicts this false theory. Our Lord and Savior Jesus Christ states, "He that is faithful in that which is least is faithful also in much" (St. Luke 16:10a).

Mrs. Ina Duley Ogden had planned her career, but was unable to proceed because of her father being an invalid. She had hoped to reach the multitudes, but now she had only one to work with. There was a transition from resentment to quiet acceptance that was rapid. As she did her household duties she came to a state of enthusiastic delight in the common work at home. As a result of her thwarted ambition, Mrs. Ogdon was enabled to write,

Do not wait until some deed of greatness you may do.
Do not wait to shed your light afar.
To the many duties ever near you now be true.
Brighten the corner where you are.

More than twenty-five million reproductions of "Brighten the Corner" have been made in hymn books, radio transcriptions, phonograph records and moving pictures. (George W. Sanville, *Forty Gospel Hymn Stories*, Winona Lake, IN: Rodeheaver-Hall Mack Co., 1943.)

The above account is just one example of how God stands ready to bless far beyond our expectation as we are faithful and willing to accept our call. It is sometimes thought of as lowly service, but treasured in the sight of God. So, let us rejoice, praise God, and be thankful wherever God has placed us in His great harvest field. The Psalmist testified, "I had rather be a doorkeeper in the house of my God, than to dwell in the tents of wickedness" (Psalm 84:10b).

As for my personal testimony, figuratively speaking, I am content to be "the hewer of thy wood unto the drawer of thy water" (Deuteronomy 29:11b) while the Temple of our God is being constructed.

May we all remember the lesson Jesus taught us concerning acceptable service in the sight of God. He accepted the slave's work and washed the feet of his disciples. In this act, Jesus gives us an example of humble service that pleases God. With this in mind, let us be willing and glad to be a "love slave" as we cooperate with God in the building of his church.

What follows in this book is written to encourage the multitude of Spirit filled Christians who serve God behind the scenes with no recognition in this world. But they look forward to God's promise in Malachi 3:17, "And they shall be mine, saith the Lord of hosts, in that day when I make up my jewels; and I will spare them, as a man spareth his own son that serveth him."

—LLOYD D. GRIMM, JR.

1
A Cup of Cold Water

"And whosoever shall give to drink unto one of these little ones a cup of cold water only in the name of a disciple, verily I say unto you, he shall in no wise lose his reward" (St. Matthew 10:42).

As WE STUDY THIS teaching of Christ, let us again remember that which was spoken by our Lord and Savior in the Gospel of St. Luke, "He that is faithful in that which is least is faithful also in much: and he that is unjust in the least is unjust also in much" (St. Luke 16:10).

Most of us will never have an opportunity to perform some great heroic deed that will be published far and wide. As followers of the lowly Nazarene, the praise and honor that comes from man should not be the motivating force for good works in the lives of God's people. Sometimes we are honored, but this honor should be immediately transferred to our Lord Jesus Christ, remembering, "So likewise ye, when ye shall have done all those things which are commanded you, say, We are unprofitable servants: we have done that which was our duty to do" (St. Luke 17:10).

Paul and Barnabas give us an example of how we should react when honor comes that is not solicited. While ministering at Lystra, these men came into contact with a man who had been crippled from the time of his birth. Paul "said with a loud voice, Stand upright on thy feet. And he leaped and walked" (Acts 14:10). The people of Lystra mistakenly took these saintly men for gods and were ready to worship them. "Which when the apostles, Barnabas and Paul, heard of, they rent their clothes, and ran in among the people, crying out, And saying, Sirs, why do ye these things? We also are men of like passions with you, and preach unto you that ye should turn from these vanities unto the living God, which made heaven, and earth, and the sea, and all things that are therein" (Acts 14:14-15). Here we see how any honor that comes from men should be returned to our Lord, who was responsible for it in the first place. The honor that comes from man should not, and need not, deter us in our good works, so long as we walk humbly with our Master.

With this in mind, let us look at what Jesus says about giving a cup of cold water. Our Lord speaks of the recipient as a "little one." There is a difference of opinion as to who Jesus means by little ones. Some think he refers to the less known disciples. Others think Jesus is speaking of little children. Still others think he has in mind new converts. However, the word least causes us to think of weakness as used elsewhere in the Word of God. For instance, when the disciples were reasoning among themselves who would be the greatest, we read, "And Jesus, perceiving the thought of their heart, took a child, and set him by him, And said unto them, Whosoever shall receive this child in my name receiveth me: and whosoever shall receive me receiveth him that sent me: for he that is least among you all, the same shall be great" (St. Luke 9:47-48).

The bottom line is not the size of our work in God's vineyard, but our being willing to follow God's plan. This being true, we will be glad to serve our entire life as a "love slave" working behind the scene, not seen by men, but because we love our Master who loved us and gave His life in order to redeem us from destruction.

I well remember a young boy I had in one of my early pastorates. Eddie lived near the church. One day I was busy mowing the church lawn when this boy appeared with water for me. Most of us had very little to give at the age of Eddie, but he gave something to me that was worth more than silver or gold.

So let us all go forth and do what we are able to do as disciples of Christ. Then on The Judgment Day, when Christ mentions the good treatment he received from his own on earth, and we fail to recall these deeds, Jesus will say, "Verily I say unto you, Inasmuch as ye have done it unto one of the least of these my brethren, ye have done it unto me" (St. Matthew 25:40b).

2

A GIFT WITH ETERNAL SIGNIFICANCE

"And being in Bethany in the house of Simon the leper, as he sat at meat, there came a woman having an alabaster box of ointment of spikenard very precious; and she brake the box, and poured it on his head. And there were some that had indignation within themselves, and said, Why was this waste of the ointment made? For it might have been sold for more than three hundred pence, and have been given to the poor. And they murmured against her. And Jesus said, Let her alone; why trouble ye her? she hath wrought a good work on me. For ye have the poor with you always, and whensoever ye will ye may do them good: but me ye have not always. She hath done what she could: she is come aforehand to anoint my body to the burying. Verily I say unto you, Wheresoever this gospel shall be preached throughout the whole world, this also that she hath done shall be spoken of for a memorial of her" (St. Mark 14:3-9).

IN READING THIS ACCOUNT, one's first impression may be that this woman was rich, and out of her abundance she gave these gifts, but on closer examination of the text we may get a clearer picture of this woman's financial status. In verse 8 Jesus says, "She hath done what she could." His statement may imply she had nothing more to give, or in modern language, she invested all she had in the stock market, choosing one company.

However, it proves her affection and genuine love for Jesus, until she was willing to become poor, following the example of Christ, as we read: "For ye know the grace of our Lord Jesus Christ, that, though he was rich, yet for your sakes he became poor, that ye through his poverty might be rich" (II Corinthians 8:9).

The God we serve is not a hard taskmaster requiring the impossible. Jesus says, "For my yoke is easy, and my burden is light" (St. Matthew 11:30).

It appears that there are many who are prone to do nothing since they have so little to invest. You may hear people say what they would do if they had the money that some have. With some, "the love of money" can become addictive. I knew a man who, if I remember correctly, was a tither, but when he got employment where his income was increased, he failed in his giving.

But we must remember that in order to be a faithful steward, there is much more involved than the giving of our tangible possessions. We all have something we can share. It may be just a smile or a few words of encouragement that will make the difference between victory or defeat to one who has become discouraged and about ready to give up the "good fight of faith."

I remember, years ago, how a man was whistling as he went about his work, and it was a blessing to me, although he was a perfect stranger. God's Word declares, "A merry heart doeth good like a medicine: but a broken spirit drieth the bones" (Proverbs 17:22). The woman in this account gave her alabaster box of precious ointment because she loved Jesus. What will you give as a token of love for our Master?

My mother was a very good cake baker, even in those days when cakes were made from scratch. She lived to be nearly ninety-nine years old. In her older years, she used this talent for others. Today, I am here in my study doing what I can by way of writing, in order to encourage God's people in our journey to heaven. I am ninety-three years old and still semi-active. I have enlisted for life in the army of God. I could twiddle my time away in useless pursuits, but I am reminded of the words of Jesus in St. John 9:4, "I must work the works of him that sent me, while it is day: the night cometh, when no man can work."

So, let us remember it is not the size of our work, but our faithfulness that counts in the sight of God. Remember what Jesus said about this woman who anointed him, "She hath done what she could" (St. Mark 14:8a). She did it before the crucifixion. We read, "She is come aforehand to anoint my body to the burying" (St. Mark 14:8b).

There are those who build up estates and leave it for a good cause, not realizing a dishonest, but shrewd attorney may find ways to change their original will. So, with so many present-day needs, it seems best to do what we can now to alleviate human suffering and spread the Gospel. "Whatsoever thy hand findeth to do, do it with thy might" (Ecclesiastes 9:10a).

3
DEDICATED YOUTH

"Now Naaman, captain of the host of the king of Syria, was a great man with his master, and honourable, because by him the Lord had given deliverance unto Syria: he was also a mighty man in valour, but he was a leper. And the Syrians had gone out by companies, and had brought away captive out of the land of Israel a little maid; and she waited on Naaman's wife. And she said unto her mistress, Would God my lord were with the prophet that is in Samaria! for he would recover him of his leprosy" (II Kings 5:1-3).

GOD WAS INTERESTED in the well-being of this heathen captain, who held a high position in the armed forces of Syria. But, the Lord had a purpose that extended far beyond the physical healing of Naaman's leprosy, and that was to show the superiority of Israel's true and living God contrasted to the false pagan gods of Syria.

In order to accomplish this goal, the Master took advantage of a time of distress in the history of Israel, for according to verse 2, the Syrians were making raids on Israel. But as so often happens, God takes the hard and difficult situations we face, as Satan works to devour us, and causes them to work for our good and His eternal glory and purpose. The Psalmist says, "Surely the wrath of man shall praise thee" (Psalms 76:10a). Romans 8:28 reads, "And we know that all things work together for good to them that love God, to them who are the called according to his purpose."

God surely turned the captivity of this little maid from Israel into a great blessing. We do not know her age, but since she is called "a little maid" we have reason to believe she was very young. Her name is not given, nor the name of her family, but she must have had very early training in the scriptures Israel had at the time of this account. Here was a young person who was solid in the faith, evidently well versed in the Word of God. The *Shema*, as recorded in Deuteronomy, holds an important place in the training of Israel's youth. It seems to condense the law and lay a firm foundation for one's faith.

This faith held her steady in a heathen environment which was not conducive to godly living, but she was steadfast in her testimony of the faith which she possessed. This little Israelite maid did not murmur or complain or become bitter in her spirit against the foreign nation that took her captive. In the providence of God, she was made an evangelist to a spiritually needy people.

The theme of this book is "Small Deeds with Eternal Significance." It was seemingly a small comment this girl made to Naaman's wife, but God used it to bring about the conversion of this great military leader of Syria. Her testimony was concise, definite, respectful and easy to be understood. She simply said, "Would God my lord were with the prophet that is in Samaria! for he would recover him of his leprosy" (II Kings 5:3b). A brief testimony given from one anointed with the Holy Spirit will draw lost souls to God. There is a scripture in the prophecy of Isaiah that should encourage every soul winner. It reads, "For as the rain cometh down, and the snow from heaven, and returneth not thither, but watereth the earth, and maketh it bring forth and bud, that it may give seed to the sower, and bread to the eater: So shall my word be that goeth forth out of my mouth: it shall not return unto me void, but it shall accomplish that which I please, and it shall prosper in the thing whereto I sent it" (Isaiah 55:10-11). Only eternity will reveal all that has been and will continue to be brought about from these few words from a young maid who loved her Lord and the lost of earth.

Young people have been, and continue to be, a driving force in God's army as we march on to victory. We see Joseph standing true to his faith though shamefully mistreated; David doing exploits for God while still a youth; the three Hebrew young people hold fast to their convictions regardless of the consequences; and young Timothy assisting the Apostle Paul in his labor. There are many others recorded in the Bible, and there are a host of modern youth today who are actively serving God.

The writer has lived over twenty-three years beyond man's allotted time on earth as recorded in God's Word. I love and appreciate young people. It is a grief to me when Christians speak of this younger generation as though the whole populace of young people have turned from God. It is true that many have turned from the faith, but to some degree it has always taken place through the ages, from what we read in history, both secular and Biblical.

While the Bible records the good deeds and dedication of many young people, the Word of God relates some of the most sordid sins of others. This is good, for it warns us to turn from evil, and encourages us to follow the good. After all, God can change bad people and give the sinner a new start. Today is Good Friday. Isn't that what Jesus Christ accomplished on that first Good Friday? Think of some that God forgave and chose to help build his kingdom, such as David, Saul of Tarsus, Zacchaeus, Matthew and many others.

We find many precious young people serving God and following the lifestyle of this little captive maid. This last winter a group of young children removed snow so we could reach our car. In old age, this kind of work becomes a burden. We felt good as a result of this kind gesture of these young people. Sometimes a child opens a door for me, and I feel encouraged to love and serve God with confidence that God still has young people in every generation who love and serve Him.

May God bless all the young people who are serving God, that they may help in saving others from the leprosy of sin.

The Apostle Paul wrote to young Timothy, "Let no man despise thy youth; but be thou an example of the believers, in word, in conversation, in charity, in spirit, in faith, in purity. Till I come, give attendance to reading, to exhortation, to doctrine. Neglect not the gift that is in thee" (I Timothy 4:12-14a).

So, we can see how this young girl, who waited on Naaman's wife, and confined as a captive, did "what she could" in spreading the gospel. To many, it would seem as having little value. But God used her few words to reach the multitudes.

Perhaps, some who read this book will feel that their environment prohibits them from active service. Remember, God's blessing on our small deeds will more than compensate for our inadequacy.

4
"HELPS" — A BIG GIFT IN DISGUISE

"And God hath set some in the church, first apostles,
secondarily prophets, thirdly teachers, after that
miracles, then gifts of healings, helps, governments,
diversities of tongues. Are all apostles? are all prophets? are all teachers? are all workers of miracles? Have
all the gifts of healing? do all speak with tongues? do
all interpret? But covet earnestly the best gifts: and
yet shew I unto you a more excellent way" (I
Corinthians 12:28-31).

FROM THIS LONG LIST of spiritual gifts, the one with
a carnal mind would probably think of the
"gift of helps" as being the least to be desired
in his or her attempt to become the greatest as a
follower of Christ. Before Pentecost, the thought of
becoming a servant, as a road leading to greatness
in the spiritual realm, was foreign in the thinking
of the disciples. Our Savior found it necessary to
correct his disciples in this matter. During a time
when they were apart from Christ, "they had dis-
puted among themselves, who should be the great-

est" (St. Mark 9:34b). We then read, "And he sat down, and called the twelve, and saith unto them, If any man desire to be first, the same shall be last of all, and servant of all" (St. Mark 9:35).

The Corinthian church prided themselves in their many gifts, failing to realize they were all given to them from the bountiful heart of God. The words of Jesus in St. John 15:5 apply here. "I am the vine, ye are the branches: He that abideth in me, and I in him, the same bringeth forth much fruit: for without me ye can do nothing." When Jesus became hungry, he saw a fig tree afar off. As he approached, our Lord found nothing but leaves. He said, "No man eat fruit of thee hereafter for ever." (See St. Mark 11:14.) The fig tree soon dried up, as we read the account, "And in the morning, as they passed by, they saw the fig tree dried up from the roots" (St. Mark 11:20).

We are thinking of helps as the gift of the Spirit. These Corinthians should have been willing to help in the least esteemed work in God's Kingdom as they remembered the cesspool of sin from which Christ had delivered them. Corinth was known for its sinfulness. If one were trying to describe a very sinful person in that day, he would say, "He lives like a Corinthian."

So just as in this Corinthian church, as all of us are indebted to Christ, and should rejoice if 'helps" is our gift in the providence of God.

But there must be a change of heart before one becomes willing to accept the lowest position in the Church of Jesus Christ. In his Word, God promises to give a change of heart to those who will unconditionally submit to his authority. The Prophet Ezekiel, under Divine inspiration, writes, "A new heart also will I give you, and a new spirit will I put within you: and I will take away the stony heart out of your flesh, and I will give you an heart of flesh. And I will put my spirit within you, and cause you to walk in my statutes, and ye shall keep my judgments, and do them" (Ezekiel 36:26-27). This change takes place when Jesus forgives us of our sins, and then tarry as the 120 did to be filled with the Holy Spirit. (See Acts 2.)

After this cleansing, these disciples had work to do. Listen to Jesus as he spoke his last words to his followers before his ascension: "But ye shall receive power, after that the Holy Ghost is come upon you: and ye shall be witnesses unto me both in Jerusalem, and in all Judæa, and in Samaria, and unto the uttermost part of the earth" (Acts 1:8).

If your gift is helps you need the baptism of the Holy Spirit, the same as those of us who are called to preach. We find this as we read the qualifications of those in God's Word who were given the gift of helps. The Early Church needed lay people to distribute food to the needy in order to relieve the apostles from this work so they could give their time "continually to prayer, and to the ministry of the word" (Acts 6:4b). Look at the description of those who were blessed with a gift of helps. These "men are of honest report, full of the Holy Ghost and wisdom" (Acts 6:3, part).

In the brief epistle of III John, we find a good man by the name of Gaius who could be taken as a pattern for one who has the gift of helps. What we know of this saint is found in this short book. It appears he was a layman, a pillar in the church, and very faithful to the cause.

There were, in those days, itinerant preachers ministering without any means of support, "Because that for his name's sake they went forth, taking nothing of the Gentiles" (III John verse 7). The Apostle John knew of one who was faithful to call on to meet this need. Knowing the character of Gaius, we can rest assured that the need was met.

Through the ages, God has always had men and

women who have been given this special gift of helps. Our generation is no exception.

Of the many I know who have been given this gift of helps, there is one who repeatedly comes to my mind. As a teenager, I had a Sunday school teacher, who, as an alcoholic, was definitely converted and filled with the Holy Spirit. He may not have had the book knowledge of many, but he was filled with the Holy Spirit. He was like those who observed Peter and John as we read in Acts 4:13, "Now when they saw the boldness of Peter and John, and perceived that they were unlearned and ignorant men, they marvelled; and they took knowledge of them, that they had been with Jesus."

When put to a severe test there are some who profess Christ, but react much like the world. But not so with this Sunday school teacher. He already had so practiced his gift of helps that he was not caught off guard when put to the test. This man of God took a genuine interest in us as teenage boys. But, the time came when he was replaced as our teacher. His reaction was a proof of his faith and love for God. His comment was brief and to the point. With his faith unshaken, he said, "Now I can bring more people to church." Here was one who taught us more by example of Christ-like living than one can ever learn from any formal book knowledge.

Surely helps is a big gift in disguise. Remember the view God has of helps, as we read in the Book of James, "Pure religion and undefiled before God and the Father is this, To visit the fatherless and widows in their affliction, and to keep himself unspotted from the world" (James 1:27).

5
RESCUED IN A BASKET

"But Saul increased the more in strength, and confounded the Jews which dwelt at Damascus, proving that this is very Christ. And after that many days were fulfilled, the Jews took counsel to kill him: But their laying await was known of Saul. And they watched the gates day and night to kill him. Then the disciples took him by night, and let him down by the wall in a basket" (Acts 9:22-25).

"And the Lord spake unto Moses, saying, See, I have called by name Bezaleel the son of Uri, the son of Hur, of the tribe of Judah: And I have filled him with the spirit of God, in wisdom, and in understanding, and in knowledge, and in all manner of workmanship" (Exodus 31:1-3).

THE APOSTLE PAUL GIVES his personal testimony of how he escaped the wrath of his persecutors by being rescued in a basket. In II Corinthians 11:32-33 we read, "In Damascus the governor under Aretas the king kept the city of the damascenes with a garrison, desirous to apprehend me: And through a window in a basket was I let down by the wall, and escaped his hands."

This was the normal way of lowering an individual by means of a rope tied to the basket. In our modern times, this means is still practiced in the Bible lands. It is the equivalent of our elevator or escalator. This method was used to lift the Prophet Jeremiah out of the dungeon. (See Jeremiah 38:7-13.)

As we read this account of the daring rescue of Paul, we are enraptured with the thought of all the means God users to deliver his own.

But in our meditation, we should also remember some of the details that so many overlook. Did you ever pause long enough to consider the man who made the rope? What if he had hastily made it out of inferior material? If that were the case, the apostle's missionary ministry could have abruptly ended. So, the rope maker, working behind the scenes, had become a part of Paul's team in reaching the lost of earth.

The theme of this writing is "Small Deeds with Eternal Significance." Whatever we do with the purpose of pleasing God will be used to glorify God and bring hope to a dying world. However small our deed, we should give our best unto the Lord. Under Divine inspiration, Paul instructed servants, saying, "And whatsoever ye do, do it heartily, as to the Lord, and not unto men" (Colossians 3:23).

In the Old Testament, God called Bezaleel and "filled him with the Spirit of God, in wisdom, and in understanding, and in knowledge, and in all manner of workmanship" (Exodus 31:3b). We cannot help noticing how similar this call was to that of the laymen called to serve tables, as recorded in Acts 6:3. God not only calls men and women into the ministry, but endows His people with special gifts, not usually thought of as a Divine call, in order to further His work. That is what took place in the calling of Bezaleel. He made use of his talents in the construction of the Temple as a house of worship in those ancient times.

God has not changed. We have different skills that God wants us to use for his purposes in building up the body of Christ's Church. "For as the body is one, and hath many members, and all the members of that one body, being many, are one body: so also is Christ" (I Corinthians 12:12).

God not only called Bezaleel, but enabled him to fulfill his mission by filling "him with the Spirit of God." This is not only a necessity in the life and work of a minister, but for all who labor in God's vineyard. One will be better in whatever profession or work he or she follows if filled with the Spirit of God.

Let us remember how God used the man who made the rope to support the Apostle Paul in his escape, thus furthering the Gospel message. So, whether our work is considered to be small or great, may we be faithful to the task God assigned to us. "He that is faithful in that which is least, is faithful also in much" (St. Luke 16:10a).

6
THE INCREASE OF SACRIFICE

"And the passover, a feast of the Jews, was nigh. When Jesus then lifted up his eyes, and saw a great company come unto him, he saith unto Philip, Whence shall we buy bread, that these may eat? And this he said to prove him: for he himself knew what he would do. Philip answered him, Two hundred pennyworth of bread is not sufficient for them, that every one of them may take a little. One of his disciples, Andrew, Simon Peter's brother, saith unto him, There is a lad here, which hath five barley loaves, and two small fishes: but what are they among so many? And Jesus said, Make the men sit down. Now there was much grass in the place. So the men sat down, in number about five thousand. And Jesus took the loaves; and when he had given thanks, he distributed to the disciples, and the disciples to them that were set down; and likewise of the fishes as much as they would. When they were filled, he said unto his disciples, Gather up the fragments that remain, that nothing be lost. Therefore they gathered them together, and filled twelve baskets with the fragments of the five barley loaves, which remained over and above unto them that had eaten" (St. John 6:4-13).

THE SCRIPTURE DOES NOT REVEAL the age of this lad, but let us assume he is a young teenager. Growing boys of that age have an appetite which requires a lot of food. It appears that this lad had provided food for his personal needs. However, it causes one to wonder why he had five barley loaves, but only two small fish. He may have been thinking if he were still hungry after eating the two small fish, he would satisfy his hunger with bread. I well remember as a growing teenager, of eating most, if not all, of a loaf of bread on one occasion.

So it would have been a real sacrifice for this lad to surrender his lunch. But we need not fear when we give our little to Jesus. For his small investment yielded a high rate of interest. This is in accord with God's promise as found in St. Luke 6:38a: "Give, and it shall be given unto you; good measure, pressed down, and shaken together, and running over, shall men give into your bosom." This promise was fulfilled when, after the multitudes had eaten, the disciples "filled twelve baskets with the fragments of the five barley loaves, which remained over and above unto them that had eaten" (St. John 6:13b). It could have been that Jesus provided enough leftovers so that each of the twelve disciples had a basket of food to take home.

Let us remember Hebrews 13:8— "Jesus Christ the same yesterday, and to day and for ever." I am amazed how God still miraculously provides for our personal needs in these modern times. I can testify to the way our Lord has met the needs of our family. In Proverbs 15:16-17 we read, "Better is little with the fear of the Lord than great treasure and trouble therewith. Better is a dinner of herbs where love is, than a stalled ox and hatred therewith." A little goes a long way when God blesses it as he did the boy's lunch. We, as stewards of God, must do our part to budget and live within our income, then we are enabled to approach God in faith for the balance of our necessities. God has not promised us a luxurious living, but he has vowed to meet our needs. We read, "But my God shall supply all your need according to his riches in glory by Christ Jesus" (Phillipians 4:19).

The Spirit filled child of God no longer needs the "toys" of this world to satisfy, for he and she are drinking from the deep well of "living water" (St. John 4:10b) that fully satisfies the thirst of the human heart. After God meets our basic need with his indwelling presence, then all small blessings of this life take on new meaning. Personally, I enjoy sitting in our yard in the cool of the evening and watch the birds as they commit themselves to the Father who cares for them. This week I looked at the heaven above. It was a clear night with the stars making a beautiful display of God's handiwork. The moon was rising, and I thought how man has walked on the surface of the moon. King David testified, "When I consider thy heavens, the work of thy fingers, the moon and the stars, which thou hast ordained; What is man, that thou art mindful of him? and the son of man, that thou visitest him?" (Psalm 8:3-4)

As children of God, these seemingly small inexpensive blessings God has provided for all, leads us to see how great our God is. Although God is in heaven, and we are on earth, yet God sees the little sparrow as it falls and cares for it. Jesus says, "Ye are of more value than many sparrows" (St. Matthew 10:31b).

We may not have much of this world to offer our Lord. But like the lad in this scripture, when we surrender what we have, God increases our capacity to enjoy the smallest blessings. I am sure this boy had all the fish and barley bread he could eat, although he shared his lunch with the great company of people who followed Jesus.

It has been many years ago, but I grew up hearing the stories and illustrations of those early holiness preachers. I well remember the one about a lady seeking the blessings of a clean heart. Of course, she desired to make a total commitment of her possessions to her Master, but she was so poor that all she owned was a washboard, evidently her means of eking out a livelihood. Then, when she gave her washboard, which was her only possession, God accepted her and filled her with His Holy Spirit. After all, God wants the surrender of our will. (See Psalm 51:16-17.)

This young lad in giving his lunch to Jesus experienced the fulfillment of God's promises as found in Proverbs 11:24. "There is that scattereth, and yet increaseth; and there is that withholdeth more than is meet, but it tendeth to poverty."

7

A SMALL INVESTMENT WITH A LARGE RETURN

"And it fell on a day, that Elisha passed to Shunem, where was a great woman; and she constrained him to eat bread. And so it was, that as oft as he passed by, he turned in thither to eat bread. And she said unto her husband, Behold now, I perceive that this is an holy man of God, which passeth by us continually. Let us make a little chamber, I pray thee, on the wall; and let us set for him there a bed, and a table, and a stool, and a candlestick: and it shall be, when he cometh to us, that he shall turn in thither" (II Kings 4:8-10). For the rest of the account, read verses 11-37 of this chapter.

God's Word speaks of this woman as being great, not because of her material possessions, but for her love of God. In his Commentary, Adam Clarke says, "Instead of great woman, the Chaldee has 'a woman fearing sin'; the Arabic, 'a woman eminent for piety before God.' This made her truly great." (Adam Clarke, *Commen-*

tary on the Bible abridged by Ralph Earle, Beacon Hill Press of Kansas City, copyright 1967.)

It appears that this husband and wife were people of means, but the scriptural account leads us to the conclusion that they were faithful stewards of that which God placed in their care. They understood the Master owned it all, and their work as faithful stewards was to improve that which they were entrusted with.

In the Parable of the Pounds (St. Luke 19:11-27), Jesus rebuked the slothful servant for doing nothing and attempting to excuse himself for his failure to show an increase in his pound. "Wherefore then gavest not thou my money into the bank, that at my coming I might have required mine own with usury?" (verse 23) The temptation is to do nothing when one has so little to invest. If we are faithful and make use of a very small talent, God will surely increase our investment, as he did with the two faithful servants by increasing their pounds two-fold.

Some years ago, one of our pastors wanted to serve a larger church. He was told to make the church larger where he was presently serving. Of course, it is God who gives the increase, but we must cooperate with God by doing our part. We who enjoy gardening know we must plow, plant, weed it, etc., although God does his part by giving us the sun and rain.

Evidently this good woman was given insight to know small investments could yield large returns. Her faithful care in meeting the needs of a weary prophet reveals her genuine stewardship of all her possessions. Perhaps, after meeting the needs of her family, she had a desire to donate the balance to the building of God's Kingdom.

We have modern day examples of such sacrifice. In the early days of our denomination, Dr. Reynolds was very active in missionary work. In the history of Nazarene missions, there is an account of this faithful steward wearing a dead man's clothing. Someone had given him money for missions plus a gift for his personal needs. He decided to give all to the work of God, then our Savior met his need. His good wife cut the dead man's suit down to his size. The shoes were too large. Someone remarked about Dr. Reynolds' large feet. He sacrificed all the humiliation for a larger return of souls. He has now no need of the large shoes and used clothing, for Dr. Reynolds now has brand new celestial clothing. May all of God's people take courage, for we read, "He that overcometh, the same shall be clothed in white raiment; and I will not blot out his name out of the book of life, but I will confess his name before my Father, and before his angels" (Revelation 3:5).

There are many we never hear of who have sacrificed the temporal for the eternal, the perishable for that which has enduring value.

From the account given us in this scripture, we see how this faithful Shunammite took little and received a huge return. She was frugal in stretching a little in order to meet the needs of many. She analyzed the prophet's needs and took care of that which was basic. She counseled with her husband, suggesting, "Let us make a little chamber, I pray thee, on the wall; and let us set for him there a bed, and a table, and a stool, and a candlestick: and it shall be, when he cometh to us, that he shall turn in thither" (II Kings 4:10). This small chamber and modest furnishings was adequate for Elisha to recline, study, meditate and be renewed for his next appointment. Think on how much more we could invest for the advancement of God's cause if we were content to do without all the luxuries, both personally and in our church buildings and equipment.

This lady was a woman of discernment. "And she said unto her husband, Behold now, I perceive that this is an holy man of God, which passeth by us continually" (II Kings 4:9). There is an unconscious influence and holy aroma that proceeds from those who are in Jesus Christ that cannot go unnoticed. Jesus says, "Ye are the light of the world. A city that is set on an hill cannot be hid" (St. Matthew 5:14). This steward of God wanted to make sure she was investing in a good cause and her small investment would yield the maximum return.

Did her small investment increase? It surely did, both for the Kingdom of God and her personal reward. Listen to what Jesus says: "He that receiveth a prophet in the name of a prophet shall receive a prophet's reward" (St. Matthew 10:41a). This woman will share in the rewards of Elisha's ministry. This truth should encourage all of God's people who labor faithfully in doing what is considered by some as insignificant, but God views as very important. On the Judgment Day we will hear Jesus say, "Verily I say unto you, Inasmuch as ye have done it unto one of the least of these my brethren, ye have done it unto me" (St. Matthew 25:40b).

8

GOD INCREASES THE TRIVIAL

"Cast thy bread upon the waters: for thou shalt find it after many days" (Ecclesiastes 11:1).

"For as the rain cometh down, and the snow from heaven, and returneth not thither, but watereth the earth, and maketh it bring forth and bud, that it may give seed to the sower, and bread to the eater: So shall my word be that goeth forth out of my mouth: it shall not return unto me void, but it shall accomplish that which I please, and it shall prosper in the thing whereto I sent it" (Isaiah 55:10-11).

THE ABOVE VERSE FROM Ecclesiastes was seemingly well known. Various interpretations have been given as to the meaning of casting our "bread upon the waters." My own personal feeling is that anything we do in faith as a disciple of Christ will not be lost, but eventually will return with a harvest. This thought is supported in scripture as we read how the Apostle Paul admonished the Corinthian Church to be generous in their support of the poor. We read, "But this I say, he which soweth sparingly shall reap also sparingly; and he which soweth bountifully shall reap also bountifully" (II Corinthians 9:6).

Let us picture a poor farmer as spring arrives, and he realizes it is time to sow. But the previous year his crops failed, leaving him with a small amount of seed, which must be divided for food and planting. His temptation would be not to sow but use it all for his immediate need, but on second thought, this farmer thought of ways by careful management to meet his present needs and by faith sow the remaining grain. He has faith to step out on the promises of God, although the present year did not look promising. However, his faith is rewarded with a bountiful harvest. God's Word reads, "There is that scattereth, and yet increaseth; and there is that withholdeth more than is meet, but it tendeth to poverty. The liberal soul shall be made fat: and he that watereth shall be watered also himself" (Proverbs 11:24-25).

The truth of this proverb can be applied in the spiritual realm in regard to soul winning. So many times, we fail to see the immediate results of our efforts in reaching the lost. It is then we must wait patiently by faith and claim the unfailing promises of God.

Years ago, a revival took place which from appearance seemed to be a failure. The one giving a report of the services mentioned how poor the revival had been, etc., then, as a matter of fact, he said that one boy was saved. Was that revival a failure? By no means! That one boy became a great General Superintendent in the Church of the Nazarene. In the early days of the denomination, Dr. R.T. Williams, with his spiritual insight, was instrumental in laying a firm foundation for this segment of building the Kingdom of God.

These modern examples of rewarded faith are an encouragement to the weary soul winner, but we need to look beyond what we see as success and stand firm on the promises of God as found in the prophecy of Isaiah quoted at the start of this chapter. In speaking of God's Word, the prophet cried out, "It shall not return unto me void" (Isaiah 55:11, part).

As laborers in God's vineyard, we should tend and be faithful to our mission rather than constantly studying the visible results. With my country background, I enjoyed gardening. But in my zeal, I know better than to go out each evening and pull up the plants and check the roots. After I have done my work, I must then wait on God to bring forth the harvest.

The Prophet Ezekiel, in his calling, was warned that he was going to a rebellious nation, but then God encouraged him by saying, "And they, whether they will hear, or whether they will forbear, (for they are a rebellious house,) yet shall know that there hath been a prophet among them" (Ezekiel 2:5).

Our work in advancing God's Kingdom is a team effort. God examines our faithfulness rather than our accomplishments. Jesus commends the two faithful servants with the same blessing, although the one was entrusted with more talents. Compare St. Matthew 25 verses 21 and 23. "His lord said unto him, Well done, thou good and faithful servant: thou hast been faithful over a few things, I will make thee ruler over many things: enter thou into the joy of thy lord."

So, let us be faithful to the talents God has entrusted us with. We may never be counted as having been successful in our chosen field of labor, but if we are faithful, God sees us in a different light. As a very young pastor, still in my twenties, I was serving a very small church. We had called an elderly evangelist for a revival. I will always remember what he said to me. "It is better to be a big man in a little place, than a little man in a big place."

"Be thou faithful unto death, and I will give thee a crown of life" (Revelation 2:10b).

9

A POOR MAN'S GIFT

"Now Peter and John went up together into the temple at the hour of prayer, being the ninth hour. And a certain man lame from his mother's womb was carried, whom they laid daily at the gate of the temple which is called Beautiful, to ask alms of them that entered into the temple; Who seeing Peter and John about to go into the temple asked an alms. And Peter, fastening his eyes upon him with John, said, Look on us. And he gave heed unto them, expecting to receive something of them. Then Peter said, Silver and gold have I none; but such as I have give I thee: In the name of Jesus Christ of Nazareth rise up and walk. And he took him by the right hand, and lifted him up: and immediately his feet and ankle bones received strength. And he leaping up stood, and walked, and entered with them into the temple, walking, and leaping, and praising God" (Acts 3:1-8).

PERHAPS THE MAJORITY OF mankind thinks of giving in terms of monetary values. However, this miracle of healing should be of encouragement to all the faithful stewards who are living in the poverty level of society, who have no tangible gift to contribute to a worthy cause, but possessed with God implanted burning desire to do something.

Here we have a man "lame from his mother's womb" (Acts 3:2, part) and now "was above forty years old" (Acts 4:22, part). His daily routine consisted of being carried to a place where he would receive alms of the compassionate people who pass by. It was a wise choice in placing this crippled man near the Temple, for it was the custom of those entering the Temple to not only have an offering, but also something for the poor.

We do not know what all was passing through the mind of the lame man as he saw Peter and John approaching. He may have been a man of quick discernment and realized that here are kind and compassionate gentlemen, for we all have an unconscious influence emanating from us, whether it be for good or evil. We see this truth being acted out in the life of Stephen during his mock trial, before he was put to death by stoning. "And all that sat in the council, looking stedfastly on him, saw his face as it had been the face of an angel" (Acts 6:15). They could not help but see the life of Jesus Christ flowing from this good man and helping to illuminate a dark and sinful world. In contrast, the sinner reveals the poison of sin flowing from his life to further lead people away from the healing found only in Jesus Christ. In the prophecy of Isaiah 3:9a we read, "The shew of their countenance doth witness against them; and they declare their sin as Sodom, they hide it not."

Then as Peter and John were "about to go into the temple" (see verse 3), this sick man asked for a donation. This account continues to unfold as we read, "And Peter, fastening his eyes upon him with John, said, Look on us. And he gave heed unto them, expecting to receive something of them" (Acts 3:4-5).

Perhaps there are various reasons why Peter said, "Look on us," but I wonder if the apostle was preparing this man for what would shock him in the next verse. Was Peter in essence saying, you see by the way we dress that we have little of this world to donate.

Then the lame man's hope of receiving a donation was dashed to pieces as Peter said, "Silver and gold have I none" (see verse 6); but quickly he saw a ray of hope as the apostle told him, "but such as I have give I thee: In the name of Jesus Christ of Nazareth rise up and walk" (see verse 6).

This poor lame man had immediate needs which must be met, but no one had ever been able to reach out to his basic need of healing, so he could provide for his own needs. Peter had no money that would purchase this man food at the market, but he had access to treasure that is foreign to the world. Peter and John were in partnership with the one who owns "the cattle upon a thousand hills" (Psalm 50:10b). We, as God's children, "have this treasure in earthen vessels." (See II Corinthians 4:7.)

In the long run, Peter and John gave this sick man a much better gift than a coin to buy his next meal. We should help with the immediate needs, but at the same time, it is important to get a man on his feet so he can provide for himself and in turn help others with the same assistance formerly shown on his behalf.

The theme of this book is "Small Deeds with Eternal Significance." Are we using what we have for the glory of God and the multitude of needy people who surround us? Peter was not able to give like Zacchaeus, who said, "Behold, Lord, the half of my goods I give to the poor" (see St. Luke 19:8). He simply stated the fact that he had nothing to give that would be accepted as far as meeting his living expenses, but quickly followed saying, "but such as I have give I thee" (see verse 6).

God will not hold us responsible for what we do not

have, but are we making full use of what he has endowed us with, even though it may be the smallest of gifts and talents? The tendency is to muse about what we would do for good if we had the ability or wealth that others possess. But, what are we doing with what we now have?

The bottom line is found in the words spoken by our Lord and Savior Jesus Christ, "He that is faithful in that which is least, is faithful also in much" (St. Luke 16:10a).

10
A Little Blessed of God

"And the word of the Lord came unto him, saying, Arise, get thee to Zarephath, which belongeth to Zidon, and dwell there: behold, I have commanded a widow woman there to sustain thee. So he arose and went to Zarephath. And when he came to the gate of the city, behold, the widow woman was there gathering of sticks: and he called to her, and said, Fetch me, I pray thee, a little water in a vessel, that I may drink. And as she was going to fetch it, he called to her, and said, Bring me, I pray thee, a morsel of bread in thine hand. And she said, As the Lord thy God liveth, I have not a cake, but an handful of meal in a barrel, and a little oil in a cruse: and, behold, I am gathering two sticks, that I may go in and dress it for me and my son, that we may eat it, and die. And Elijah said unto her, Fear not; go and do as thou hast said: but make me thereof a little cake first, and bring it unto me, and after make for thee and for thy son. For thus saith the Lord God of Israel, The barrel of meal shall not waste, neither shall the cruse of oil fail, until the day that the Lord sendeth rain upon the earth. And she went and did according to the saying of Elijah: and she, and he, and her house, did eat many days. And the barrel of meal wasted not, neither did the cruse of oil fail, according to the word of the Lord, which he spake by Elijah" (I Kings 17:8-16).

THIS MIRACLE OF SUPPLYING the needs of a poor widow and her son took place in a time in the history of Israel, when it was very difficult to eke out even a very meager existence. There was a drought, which always limits the amount of food available. But more importantly was the fact that the majority of the people had forsaken the true and living God— who had wrought great deliverance for them in former times— in order to worship and serve the false god Baal.

Yet, there were some who still held the moral standard high, and like the three Hebrew children, would rather die than to bow the knee to the false and degrading gods of this world.

The poor widow in this account was one of those in Israel who still retained her faith, although tested to the limit. This was proven by her obedient surrender to God. All her resources were exhausted with the exception of one meal. In those days, there was no public provision for charity. Her means of support would all soon be gone unless God intervened on her behalf. Her husband was deceased and we do not know that her son was old enough to be an alternate means of support. Nevertheless, both she and her son were one meal away from death by starvation.

Now, her real test comes by sacrificing her "Isaac on the altar." We all come, sooner or later, with the same test of our faith. It may not be the same as to the means used, but it is the one thing that we are tempted by Satan to not surrender. With this lady, it was her last meal. By looking at the worldly facts, it meant the death of her and her son, but her faith in God caused her to mount up and thus find deliverance.

It was this genuine faith that enabled Shadrach, Meshach and Abednego to hold firm when given a second chance to save their lives from burning. They answered by saying, "If it be so, our God whom we serve is able to deliver us from the burning fiery furnace, and he will deliver us out of thine hand, O king. But if not, be it known unto thee, O king, that we will not serve thy gods, nor worship the golden image which thou hast set up" (Daniel 3:17-18).

In these writings, may God help us to see how small deeds done as Christ's disciples have eternal significance. This widow had little to surrender, but she was not afraid to release her little to God who abundantly blessed and met her need.

I heard of a lady who said, "Oh, I would be afraid to surrender all to God." Right here is the crux of the whole matter in our unconditional surrender and permitting the Holy Spirit to take full control. We need not fear when we surrender ourselves and our families to God. It brings us a release and freedom, otherwise not known.

Many years ago, our younger son had an infection that appeared life threatening. I was doing all I could to bring about his healing only to see no improvement. Then, as with Abraham, I had my "Isaac" to offer. I remember the support of my church family that Sunday morning when I knelt at the altar and offered my "Isaac." My prayer was, "I pray for my son's healing, but I give him to you, Lord, if you want to take him home."

What was the result of that prayer? A miracle took place! That same Sunday, there was rapid improvement and soon our son was restored to health. This experience happened about fifty-nine years ago, but it still is a boost to my faith.

We may not have much to give, but God is more interested in us giving first ourselves, then all our material needs will be met. As the Apostle Paul wrote concerning giving, "And this they did, not as we hoped, but first gave their own selves to the Lord, and unto us by the will of God" (II Corinthians 8:5).

The widow planned to prepare and eat her last meal and then die. Elijah listened to her plan and replied, "Fear not; go and do as thou hast said: but make me thereof a little cake first, and bring it unto me, and after make for thee and for thy son" (I Kings 17:13b). By faith she obeyed and was rewarded. If we wait until we can see the outcome, we are no longer living by faith, but by sight. The words of Jesus Christ stand sure and settled for all eternity. "But seek ye first the kingdom of God, and his righteousness; and all these things shall be added unto you" (St. Matthew 6:33).

Furthermore, if we wait until we can see the outcome of our every move, we will accomplish very little. Sometimes, it may be an excuse for not taking action. "The slothful man saith, There is a lion in the way; a lion is in the streets" (Proverbs 26:13). This widow surely had what would be considered by most people a valid reason to keep her last meal, but her faith exceeded human reason, believing in the all sufficiency of the true and living God to provide for all her needs.

The resources of our God are inexhaustible, so bring your vessels, not a few, and God will fill them. The only thing that stopped the flow of oil for this poverty stricken woman was her inability to provide any more containers to receive the oil.

Remember, the little we have, always surrendered to God, will be blessed beyond measure. I can testify to this truth. Most of my life I have been able to live on what the world considers an inadequate salary, but when I give God first place, he stretches what I have and I feel I have plenty, because I serve the God who owns "the cattle upon a thousand hills" (Psalm 50:1b).

So, the bottom line is that what little we have, when fully surrendered to God, will be of eternal significance.

11
MAKING FULL USE OF OUR LITTLE

"And I say unto you, Make to yourselves friends of the mammon of unrighteousness; that, when ye fail, they may receive you into everlasting habitations. He that is faithful in that which is least is faithful also in much: and he that is unjust in the least is unjust also in much. If therefore ye have not been faithful in the unrighteous mammon, who will commit to your trust the true riches? And if ye have not been faithful in that which is another man's, who shall give you that which is your own?" (St. Luke 16:9-12)

IN THIS TEACHING OF our Lord, there are two prominent and very important truths that all mankind needs to heed, and act accordingly: (1) We, as human beings, own no material possessions as occupants of this world; (2) In the world to come, all Christians who have faithfully served their Master will actually be given, by the authority of God, that which is their own.

In order to get the full sense of his teaching, one needs to study the context of that which precedes and which follows these four verses. (Read Luke 16.) We read of the shrewd steward who wasted his master's goods (verse 1) and cunningly conceived of a plan to cover up his embezzlement. In verse 9, Jesus is not condoning this sinful man or his foresight, but delivering a deeper spiritual analogy that all the children of God need to remember. This administrator, spiritually speaking, represents all those who are seeking for a cheap religion. They are like Balaam, who tried to compromise and grasp both this world and heaven, allowing his plan to backfire. In the process, it appears he lost both worlds.

God's Word teaches, and experience supports, the fact that we, as human beings, do not own the material possessions that have been entrusted to our care and development. God is owner, while man is steward.

This being true, we should hold loosely all in our control. We are uncertain as to the time when all, sooner or later, will hear those words from our Master and owner, "give an account of thy stewardship; for thou mayest be no longer steward" (St. Luke 16:2b).

That day in which we must report the way we handled our stewardship may be sooner than we anticipate. Years ago, in one of my pastorates, there was a husband and wife, who Satan deceived and drew them away from their Christian endeavor. They lived in an area where it was conducive to develop a resort. What started out as a family affair, ended in robbing these people of their greatest possession, being their spiritual experience. The family project became a thriving business. Their church attendance ceased, since they kept their business open on the Lord's Day. They continued to be good moral people, but out of victory.

Finally, they gave up their project that had sidetracked them from serving God. This husband now was living for God as he went to the physician for a checkup. This took place many years ago, but I clearly remember him telling me he was in perfect health, but about two days later this steward was called to give an account of his stewardship. How close this man came to the "second death" from which there is no recovery. "He that overcometh shall not be hurt of the second death" (Revelation 2:11b). But think of the wasted time that could have been used for the building of God's Kingdom.

As I remember, these folks wanted to get out of this business, evidently in order to get back to serving God. They put it up for sale, but there were no buyers. Finally, they decided to close it even though it was not sold, and almost immediately the business sold. We cannot barter with God. Those people had to come to the place where they, like the three Hebrew children, were going to serve God even if there was no deliverance.

Making money in order to become rich should never be a goal in itself. The Bible standard is found in Psalm 62:10b, which reads, "If riches increase, set not your heart upon them." I remember our late district superintendent, Dr. Harvey S. Galloway, saying that God has given some the talent to make money. Of course, he was teaching of our use of what God has blessed us with.

The Apostle Paul, in writing to young Timothy, said to "Charge them that are rich in this world, that they be not highminded, nor trust in uncertain riches, but in the living God, who giveth us richly all things to enjoy; That they do good, that they be rich in good works, ready to distribute, willing to communicate; Laying up in store for themselves a good foundation against the time to come, that they may lay hold on eternal life" (I Timothy 6:17-19).

It is certain we cannot take anything of this world with us, but we can send the good use of it to heaven before we arrive. That is what Jesus is referring to in St. Luke 16:9, "And I say unto you, Make to yourselves friends of the mammon of unrighteousness; that, when ye fail, they may receive you into everlasting habitations." In other words, use your money to win souls, so that when you fail or die, there will be people in heaven who outrun you in the race, but waiting inside those heavenly gates to welcome you, all because you used your wealth to save them and not for unprofitable selfish pursuits.

Our stewardship includes all our talents, gifts, possessions, etc. Whether we have been endowed with few or many talents, the fact remains that our all must be unconditionally surrendered to God. I heard a good man giving public testimony, saying he had a goal of becoming a millionaire. I knew this individual for years. He worked for God and has been a blessing to many, but according to God's Word, riches are given to some in order to use for good as God leads. I feel this man really was a man of God, but for some unknown reason, the truth of the scriptures had not penetrated his mind. I feel sure he is in heaven.

But we must all be careful and search the scriptures in order that we do not rationalize away the clear truth of God's Word to our destruction. The title of this chapter is "Making Full Use of Our Little." The Adversary will attempt to deceive people who have little to offer to do nothing as stewards of what they have. In the parable of talents (St. Matthew 25), the man with one talent made no use of it, but only tried to give excuses for his neglect.

If we have just one talent, then let us make full use of the same. When thinking of stewardship, our minds turn to money, but much more is included as we think of our time, talents, gifts, helps, etc.

The bottom line is to know God in his fullness and be faithful unto death. Then God will give us that which will be our own.

"He that is faithful in that which is least is faithful also in much" (St. Luke 16:10a).

"And if ye have not been faithful in that which is another man's, who shall give you that which is your own?" (St. Luke 16:12)

12
A SANCTIFIED SEAMSTRESS

"Now there was at Joppa a certain disciple named
Tabitha, which by interpretation is called Dorcas: this
woman was full of good works and almsdeeds which
she did. And it came to pass in those days, that she
was sick, and died: whom when they had washed,
they laid her in an upper chamber. And forasmuch
as Lydda was nigh to Joppa, and the disciples had
heard that Peter was there, they sent unto him two
men, desiring him that he would not delay to come
to them. Then Peter arose and went with them. When
he was come, they brought him into the upper chamber: and all the widows stood by him weeping, and
shewing the coats and garments which Dorcas made,
while she was with them. But Peter put them all forth,
and kneeled down, and prayed; and turning him to
the body said, Tabitha, arise. And she opened her eyes:
and when she saw Peter, she sat up. And he gave her
his hand, and lifted her up, and when he had called
the saints and widows, presented her alive. And it
was known throughout all Joppa; and many believed
in the Lord" (Act 9:36-42).

IN THIS PASSAGE OF scripture, we have a portrait of an early century saint of God by the name of Tabitha. In the Aramaic her name is Tabitha, but translated into the Greek she is known as Dorcas. In the Bible, names were given which were suitable to one's character. For instance, God changed Abram's name to Abraham, saying, "Neither shall thy name any more be called Abram, but thy name shall be Abraham; for a father of many nations have I made thee" (Genesis 17:5).

In like manner, Dorcas had a name which matched the saintly life she experienced. The name actually is defined "gazelle," or meaning a beautiful swift animal. Dorcas was swift in "good works and almsdeeds which she did" (Acts 9:36b).

The Bible does not describe or mention about any physical beauty as it does in a case of Rachel (see Genesis 29:17). But, Dorcas had a beauty of moral excellence that exceeded any passing physical beauty, as far as time compared to eternity.

The life of a widow was very difficult in ancient times. There was no public assistance provided for the poor, as we have in our country today. Their first means of support was their family, but if the husband and sons were deceased, as in the case of Naomi, then they would be left desolate without any help, except that which was donated by kind, benevolent individuals acting singularly or collectively as practiced by the Early Christian Church (see Acts 6:1-7).

One commentator says that Dorcas was rich. I do not know his source of information, but since the Bible is silent as to her financial status, we will proceed assuming that Dorcas was a member of the support group of widows who had come to mourn her departure.

God's Word does not go into the details of her life, but much can be known and learned from the brief description of what is recorded in verse 36b, "this woman was full of good works and almsdeeds which she did."

It appears Dorcas was using her God given talent to glorify God by meeting her needs and that of others, even as the Apostle Paul made use of his skills as a tent maker. This seamstress gave heed to God's Word as found in Ecclesiastes 9:10a where we read, "Whatsoever thy hand findeth to do, do it with thy might." She did not wait for more profitable works, but made good use of that which was now available, even as the woman who gave her alabaster box of ointment to Jesus. Our Savior said, "She hath done what she could" (St. Mark 14:8a).

This saintly lady appears to have died right in the midst of her usefulness. Recently, I met a minister who believed God promised a long life to all of his children. He gave scripture for his assumption, and that is good. I believe the scriptures the same as this good man does. One of the various scriptures relating to this promise is found in Ephesians 6:2-3, which reads, "Honour thy father and mother; which is the first commandment with promise; That it may be well with thee, and thou mayest live long on the earth." In our following discussion, I related how these promises have a general application. I told this minister that I know of many Spirit-filled Christians who have died young. We need to compare scripture with scripture in concluding what the Bible teaches on a given subject. I give just one of many scriptures that bear on this thought, found in Isaiah 57:1-2: "The righteous perisheth, and no man layeth it to heart: and merciful men are taken away, none considering that the righteous is taken away from the evil to come. He shall enter into peace: they shall rest in their beds, each one walking in his uprightness."

Dorcas died, but her influence for good continued. Like Abel, "he being dead yet speaketh" (Hebrews 11:4b). Even so, it was true of Dorcas. In verse 39, the widows were showing Peter "the coats and garments which Dorcas made, while she was with them." In Proverbs 13:22a, we read, "A good man leaveth an inheritance to his children's children." This good woman left tangible gifts of garments and coats in order to relieve the temporal suffering of mankind, but she left a much greater spiritual heredity in her influence for good.

Because of this good sanctified seamstress, Dorcas sewing circles were formed for the needs of the poor. Her little needle and thread appear small, but continue to make an eternal significance. Whatever reference the following scripture has to future events, the basic truth can be applied to the life of Dorcas and all true followers of our Lord Jesus Christ: "And I heard a voice from heaven saying unto me, Write, Blessed are the dead which die in the Lord from henceforth: Yea, saith the Spirit, that they may rest from their labours; and their works do follow them" (Revelation 14:13).

13
GOD'S EVALUATION OF A GIFT

"And Jesus sat over against the treasury, and beheld how the people cast money into the treasury: and many that were rich cast in much. And there came a certain poor widow, and she threw in two mites, which make a farthing. And he called unto him his disciples, and saith unto them, Verily I say unto you, That this poor widow hath cast more in, than all they which have cast into the treasury: For all they did cast in of their abundance; but she of her want did cast in all that she had, even all her living" (St. Mark 12:41-44).

HERE, WE HAVE ANOTHER account of a poor widow, out of love, giving a very small offering. But according to Jesus, it was the largest donation given on that particular occasion, not because of its value, but the motive which prompted her to sacrifice all her living.

It was no sacrifice for the rich to make large donations, for Jesus says, "For all they did cast in of their abundance" (St. Mark 12:44a). But this widow cast into the treasury her entire livelihood, which was proof of her surrendered will to God.

Somewhere, I read a little story which we should ponder as we study this passage of scripture. A conversation was taking place between a pig and a chicken concerning a breakfast which was going to take place. The menu would be bacon and eggs. The hen said she would contribute the eggs. The hog mentioned that he would provide the bacon, then said to the hen that her eggs were a donation, but his giving would be a sacrifice.

Even so, there are those with us today that are financially able to give large donations, and it hardly makes a dent in their wealth. And like this widow, there are those who have little, but are willing to sacrifice for the needs that God reveals to them.

When I was in school preparing for the ministry, there was a young lady who had such a passion for missions, that she gave all her money when the offering was received. She, like the widow, gave her all. It was a very little donation, but was a genuine sacrifice. I was relating this event to one who said that this student might as well give all her money, for she didn't have enough to do her any good. But Jesus views these small gifts differently, even as He did the widow's two mites.

Our love for our Lord Jesus Christ and humanity should be the only motivating force for our work in building God's Kingdom.

Regardless of our financial position, we must remember that the true and living God owns all, even ourselves. This truth is clearly stated in I Corinthians 6:19-20, where we read, "What? know ye not that your body is the temple of the Holy Ghost which is in you, which ye have of God, and ye are not your own? For ye are bought with a price: therefore glorify God in your body, and in your spirit, which are God's."

The First Century Church put this truth into action,

for when a need arose, in order to meet that need, the entire church sacrificed all the property they possessed. We read, "And the multitude of them that believed were of one heart and of one soul: neither said any of them that ought of the things which he possessed was his own; but they had all things common" (Acts 4:32).

Then in the same chapter, we continue to read in verses 34 and 35, "Neither was there any among them that lacked: for as many as were possessors of lands or houses sold them, and brought the prices of the things that were sold, And laid them down at the apostles' feet: and distribution was made unto every man according as he had need."

The spirit of this practice is as relevant today as it was in that day. It is not a matter of being rich or poor, but of being unconditionally and totally surrendered to the will of God.

John Wesley is known for his teaching concerning stewardship by saying, "Make all you can, save all you can, and give all you can." This great man of God surely practiced what he preached. Wesley carried a burden, not only for the spiritual needs of humanity, but also for the suffering poor. As he sat in his study, viewing the pictures on the wall, he thought about the needs of the people. With that thought in mind, he reasoned how he could sell his pictures and give the proceeds to the poor.

How much luxury, if any, should we possess when never-dying souls are starving to death, both spiritually and physically. In Acts 20:35, God's Word reads, "I have shewed you all things, how that so labouring ye ought to support the weak, and to remember the words of the Lord Jesus, how he said, It is more blessed to give than to receive." Also, the Master says, "And he said unto them, Take heed, and beware of covetousness: for a man's life consisteth not in the abundance of the things which he possesseth" (St. Luke 12:15).

This poor widow is now in a better world, where wealth is not calculated by the amount of gold, silver or investments one temporally possesses.

The matter of stewardship is not confined merely to the rich, but to all ranks of people. Personally, most of my life I have been on a limited income, but I still need to be a good steward of what I have. I used to wonder if my giving was the correct amount in God's sight. I can testify that a wonderful release or freedom comes when we fully realize God owns it all, and for a little while I am only responsible for the use of what already belongs to God. While I have practiced good stewardship through all my life, I was set free of the bondage I had concerning my giving when I ceased to struggle as to the details of my donations, realizing what I have is God's. I already had given my all to God, but now I have a deeper understanding of being God's steward.

I have a word of caution for all who are making donations to charity and various appeals. Some are genuine causes, while some are false. We live in a day when our telephones are constantly used as a means of soliciting donations. As faithful stewards, we should be careful in appeals, even of the religious nature. One lady asked for prayer from a certain religious faith, and was told she must pay them $100.00. Then, she requested prayer from another organization and they took her prayer request, not asking for anything. There was a lady from one of our churches who was approached by two strangers and was swindled out of about $9,000.00.

We should not use these experiences as an excuse for doing nothing, but make careful inquiries and fully investigate as to the genuineness of the cause.

May we be so true and faithful as stewards, that when we are called to give an account of our stewardship (see

St. Luke 16:1-13), we can answer humbly, but with the assurance from God that we have done what we could.

"Be thou faithful unto death, and I will give thee a crown of life" (Revelation 2:10b).

14
UNCONDITIONAL SURRENDER

"And again the anger of the Lord was kindled against Israel, and he moved David against them to say, Go, number Israel and Judah. And Joab said unto the king, Now the Lord thy God add unto the people, how many soever they be, an hundredfold, and that the eyes of my lord the king may see it: but why doth my lord the king delight in this thing? And David's heart smote him after that he had numbered the people. And David said unto the Lord, I have sinned greatly in that I have done: and now, I beseech thee, O Lord, take away the iniquity of thy servant; for I have done very foolishly. And Gad came that day to David, and said unto him, Go up, rear an altar unto the Lord in the threshingfloor of Araunah the Jebusite. And David, according to the saying of Gad, went up as the Lord commanded. And Araunah said, Wherefore is my lord the king come to his servant? And David said, To buy the threshingfloor of thee, to build an altar unto the Lord, that the plague may be stayed from the people. And Araunah said unto David, Let my lord the king take and offer up what seemeth good unto him: behold, here be oxen for burnt sacrifice, and threshing instruments and other instruments of the oxen for wood. All these things did Araunah, as a king, give unto the king. And the king said unto Araunah, Nay; but I will surely buy it of thee at a price: neither will I offer burnt offerings unto the Lord my God of that which doth cost me nothing. And David built there an altar unto the Lord, and offered burnt offerings and peace offerings. So the Lord was intreated for the land, and the plague was stayed from Israel" (II Samuel 24, part).

I N THIS DIALOGUE WE HAVE a portrayal of another individual who was totally and unconditionally surrendered to the perfect and undivided will of God. All we know of Araunah is to be found in this chapter and I Chronicles 21, but there is enough to speak volumes concerning the character of this good man.

This account mentions no special gifts or talents that Araunah was blessed with, but he had what was necessary in order to provide an atonement for the sin of King David, thus removing the plague from Israel.

His giving was not a cup of cold water, but making it possible for God to give that "well of water springing up into everlasting life" (St. John 4:14b).

So, he may not have been gifted with special gifts that draw the praise and admiration of men, but he was glad to work behind the scenes, and be a silent partner in building the Kingdom of God.

It could have been that he had no money to donate in order to purchase sacrificial animals for the necessary sacrifice, but by becoming a "living sacrifice" (see Romans 12:11), Araunah cooperated with God's plan to forgive the sin of King David, and restore peace to the nation.

King David was motivated by an impulse from Satan to number the men of Israel and Judah who were fit for military service. In II Samuel 24:1 we could easily misinterpret the sense as it reads, "And again the anger of the Lord was kindled against Israel, and he moved David against them to say, Go, number Israel and Judah." God's Kingdom is not divided and in no way could or would God punish others for what he had planned. Again, we need to read all God's Word on a given subject, then by God's Holy Spirit guiding us, come to the clear meaning. With this in mind, turn to the parallel passage found in I Chronicles 21:1, which reads, "And Satan stood up against Israel, and provoked David to number Israel." Also, we read in James 1:13, "Let no man say when he is tempted, I am tempted of God: for God cannot be tempted with evil, neither tempteth he any man:" So, we see it was Satan who tempted King David and not God.

The judgment that followed this act of disobedience on the part of David was the natural consequence of sin in God's moral universe. Often, the righteous suffer (see verse 17), because of the sins of the guilty. With our finite minds, we will never understand all the providence of God that comes to us as we make our journey to heaven; so we need to commit those things to God, realizing he has our best interests in view, and eventually make up for all our loss and suffering we experience in this life.

When Araunah realized what was happening to God's people as a result of sin, he was not willing to stand by and take no action. A sacrifice had to be made in order to stay the judgment that had begun to take place.

As we continue to think about small deeds with eternal significance, the question may come concerning how this applies in the life of Araunah. The king told Araunah that he had come, "To buy the threshingfloor of thee, to build an altar unto the Lord, that the plague may be stayed from the people" (II Samuel 24:21b). In the following verse, Araunah was so surrendered to God and his cause that he not only gave up his threshing floor, but whatever else was necessary in order to make atonement for the sin of David. In the account in I Chronicles 21:23b, Araunah said, "I give it all."

It appears Araunah may have not had any cash to donate in order to purchase the sacrificial animals, etc., but was determined to find a way he could help bring a revival and healing to the nation. In this case, his total sacrifice would reduce him to a state of poverty, as he even gave up his means of providing a living.

The result of this good man's sacrifice and cooperation in God's plan to make an atonement for this act of sin was that revival came and the land was healed. The passage concludes, "And David built there an altar unto the Lord, and offered burnt offerings and peace offerings. So the Lord was intreated for the land, and the plague was stayed from Israel" (II Samuel 24:25).

Let us not wait until we can accomplish some great deed, but be alert, and like Araunah, be willing to give all, if necessary, in order to relieve the spiritual and physical suffering of those we come in contact with on a continual daily basis.

15
THE GIFT OF SUPPORT (ENCOURAGEMENT)

"I have coveted no man's silver, or gold, or apparel. Yea, ye yourselves know, that these hands have ministered unto my necessities, and to them that were with me. I have shewed you all things, how that so labouring ye ought to support the weak, and to remember the words of the Lord Jesus, how he said, It is more blessed to give than to receive" (Acts 20:33-35).

"Now we exhort you, brethren, warn them that are unruly, comfort the feebleminded, support the weak, be patient toward all men" (I Thessalonians 5:14).

THESE TWO SCRIPTURES taken together teach us that we have a responsibility to support those in need, both physical and spiritual.

Here, in his parting words and testimony to his grieving friends, the Apostle Paul relates how he worked in order, not only to supply his personal needs, but also in order to meet the necessities of others.

The word support is not limited to physical needs, but has a broader meaning. It conveys the idea of upholding that which is falling. It is in this sense I will write of the little things we are capable of doing to encourage and support others and keep them from falling into "the snare of the devil" (I Timothy 3:7b).

One of the best means of support comes by way of encouragement. The word *encouragement* is not listed as one of the gifts of the Spirit, at least in the King James Version, but I feel sure it is a gift of the Spirit, since helps is one of the gifts mentioned. As one studies the meaning of the word *helps*, he or she will readily conclude that encouragement is definitely a gift of the Spirit.

Also, we will find how important this gift is as we read how God's people were exhorted to encourage one another. In the prophecy of Isaiah 41:6-7, we read, "They helped every one his neighbour; and every one said to his brother, Be of good courage. So the carpenter encouraged the goldsmith, and he that smootheth with the hammer him that smote the anvil, saying, It is ready for the sodering: and he fastened it with nails, that it should not be moved."

In this passage of scripture we see how it took a team effort to bring the finished project to completion. So it is in building the Kingdom of God. These people were not self-centered, but encouraged those working in skills which they did not possess, in order to reach a common goal. Sometimes, just a word of encouragement or a smile may give courage to one who is about to falter and give up "the good fight of faith." Dr. E.O. Chalfant, who years ago was District Superintendent of our Chicago Central District, said that he "would 'amen' a young preacher even if he were saying nothing." I am sure he didn't mean he would flatter a person, but that he would find something he could say "amen" to, and thus encourage him. It is interesting, as well as instructive, how we find something good to say at the funeral of one who was known as a very wicked individual during his or her lifetime. How good and profitable it would be if these good words were spoken while one was alive in this world. It could make the difference in one's eternal destiny.

Years ago, on one of our districts, we had a good, genuine minister who would sit by himself in a group setting. He was known as a "lone wolf," although with a little research, he should not have been labeled as such. Then, the time came when God sent an angel band in order to carry him home to his reward. I feel he was escorted to one of the most prominent seats in heaven. After his death, his wife told how he was born out of wedlock and felt he was not worthy to sit with others. If only there had been someone who had developed a close friendship with this pastor and had encouraged him by showing that God loved him regardless of his background. It would have, no doubt, greatly impacted his life. We are only responsible for what we do concerning our own sins. In Jeremiah 31:29-30, one reads, "In those days they shall say no more, The fathers have eaten a sour grape, and the children's teeth are set on edge. But every one shall die for his own iniquity: every man that eateth the sour grape, his teeth shall be set on edge."

Moses was forbidden to lead the children of Israel into the Promised Land because of his disobedience in striking the rock to bring forth water. Two times God called on Moses to bring water out of the rock. The first time, he was to perform this miracle by striking the rock, which was in obedience to God's will. The second time he was just to speak to the rock, but Moses, this time in disobedience to God's will, struck the rock twice. (See Numbers 20:7-12.) Consequently, he was not permitted to take Israel into that good land flowing with milk and honey, which is a type of the life of Holiness. In Deuteronomy 1:37-38, it is recorded, "Also the Lord was angry with me for your sakes, saying, Thou also shalt not go in thither. But Joshua the son of Nun, which standeth before thee, he shall go in thither: encourage him: for he shall cause Israel to inherit it."

Moses no longer had the privilege of leading God's people into Canaan land, yet he had something he could do in order to advance God's purpose by way of encouraging Joshua, who replaced him. The Kingdom of God would go forward much more rapidly if His people were not interested in who gets the earthly credit for the deed performed.

In fact, Jesus says, "But when thou doest alms, let not thy left hand know what thy right hand doeth: That thine alms may be in secret: and thy Father which seeth in secret himself shall reward thee openly" (St. Matthew 6:3-4). In the preceding verse 2b, our Lord informs us if we do good deeds for the earthly praise of men, we have already received our reward in full: "How can ye believe, which receive honour one of another, and seek not the honour that cometh from God only?" (St. John 5:44)

As I mentioned from time to time, one must read the entire Bible, comparing scripture with scripture, in order to conclude the meaning of a given subject.

In Hebrews 10:24, the inspired Word of God reads, "And let us consider one another to provoke unto love and to good works." Adam Clarke, the early Methodist commentator, says that the word *provocation* is often taken in a good sense. It is used here as a means of doing good in order to excite or stir others to follow our example. The Apostle Paul exhorted the Corinthians, "Be ye followers of me, even as I also am of Christ" (I Corinthians 11:1).

It all depends on our motive, or we could say, "What prompts us in performing a good work?" Is it for self or for God's glory and a means of stirring others to follow our example, as we see in St. Paul's challenge to the Corinthian church?

I have been inspired by the example of a lady from the church I attended before my days as a pastor. This incident took place many years ago, during the infancy of our denomination. This good woman had saved money in order to purchase a coat. I am not sure of the need that arose, but I think it was for foreign missionary work. She effectively sacrificed her coat as she contributed her savings for this spiritual need. Such sacrifices inspire me to follow the example of those saints as they followed Christ.

Sometimes we can apply the gift of encouragement to our personal wellbeing as David did, "And David was greatly distressed; for the people spake of stoning him, because the soul of all the people was grieved, every man for his sons and for his daughters: but David encouraged himself in the Lord his God" (I Samuel 30:6). Also, in Psalms 42 and 43, King David takes inventory of his soul, looking at himself objectively, and cries out, "Why art thou cast down, O my soul? and why art thou disquieted in me? hope thou in God: for I shall yet praise him for the help of his countenance" (Psalm 42:5). He repeated almost the identical words in the concluding verse of this Psalm and in Psalm 43:5.

So it is not necessarily an indication that our mind is slipping if we occasionally talk to ourselves, for it appears King David did. David was here working through his problem in a close partnership with God (see Psalm 43:5). Perhaps David was close to God in prayer as he asks this question.

This gift of support can be practiced in many ways. The theme of this book is, "Small Deeds with Eternal Significance." Most of our good deeds will be the many seemingly little things we can do to support and encourage people to follow Jesus Christ during our brief probation on earth. You may be the one God will use to restore color to the fading cheeks of one who has become discouraged. "Let him know, that he which converteth the sinner from the error of his way shall save a soul from death, and shall hide a multitude of sins" (James 5:20).

16

LOVE, THE CAP SHEAF OF OUR LABOR

"Now ye are the body of Christ, and members in particular. And God hath set some in the church, first apostles, secondarily prophets, thirdly teachers, after that miracles, then gifts of healings, helps, governments, diversities of tongues. Are all apostles? are all prophets? are all teachers? are all workers of miracles? Have all the gifts of healing? do all speak with tongues? do all interpret? But covet earnestly the best gifts: and yet shew I unto you a more excellent way. Though I speak with the tongues of men and of angels, and have not charity, I am become as sounding brass, or a tinkling cymbal. And now abideth faith, hope, charity, these three; but the greatest of these is charity" (I Corinthians 12:27-31; 13:1, 13).

I REVERT TO MY EARLY DAYS when I worked on my grandfather's farm, in order to get a fitting title for this last chapter. The binder, or reaper, was a machine that would cut the grain, tie the wheat in bundles, or sheaves, and cast them out. These sheaves were placed together making a shock of wheat. Then the farmer would take what was known as the cap sheaf and placed it on the top of the shock for the protection of the grain. In the same manner, charity, or love as some translate the word, is the cap sheaf in order to complete the Christian's labors as he or she is employed in the Master's harvest.

The Corinthian church appears to have taken pride in their talents and gifts, but were lacking in that perfect love as described in this 13th chapter of I Corinthians.

They failed to realize that all their gifts were given to them by God. "And God hath set some in the church" (I Corinthians 12:28a). Then we read of some gifts God had bestowed on the church. These people were not ready to make full use of their gifts for they were yet carnal. Notice I Corinthians 3:1— "And I, brethren, could not speak unto you as unto spiritual, but as unto carnal, even as unto babes in Christ."

It is a sobering thought when we remember the teaching of God's Word that our good works may not pass on the Day of Judgment. The Apostle Paul warns the Corinthian church and all of this very real danger. "Every man's work shall be made manifest: for the day shall declare it, because it shall be revealed by fire; and the fire shall try every man's work of what sort it is. If any man's work abide which he hath built thereupon, he shall receive a reward. If any man's work shall be burned, he shall suffer loss: but he himself shall be saved; yet so as by fire" (I Corinthians 3:13-15).

There are various interpretations of the scripture. It appears to teach that there are those who are sincere, but mistakenly instruct and preach doctrines contrary to the truth. Even so, it teaches that all of our good works will be judged by the motive of the heart, which should be sincere love to God and man. This truth is relevant in using our spiritual gifts as we labor in the building of God's Kingdom. The young aspiring pastor who works hard to build his small congregation in order that he will be promoted is guilty of this danger.

Then, there are those who love the praise of men. Listen to our Lord Jesus Christ as he preaches, "Take heed that ye do not your alms before men, to be seen of them: otherwise ye have no reward of your Father which is in heaven. Therefore when thou doest thine alms, do not sound a trumpet before thee, as the hypocrites do in the synagogues and in the streets, that they may have glory of men. Verily I say unto you, They have their reward. But when thou doest alms, let not thy left hand know what thy right hand doeth: That thine alms may be in secret: and thy Father which seeth in secret himself shall reward thee openly" (St. Matthew 6:1-4).

Here Jesus mentions how the hypocrites would take a trumpet and blow it in order to get the attention of the people, then do a good work in order to receive the glory of men.

All glory belongs to God. The Bible has many references to this truth. In Psalm 29:12 we read, "Give unto the Lord, O ye mighty, give unto the Lord glory and strength. Give unto the Lord the glory due unto his name; worship the Lord in the beauty of holiness."

I am hesitant as I write about a personal conviction, for it is not my goal to force my personal feeling on good people who feel led in a different direction. It has become a custom in many of our churches to applaud after one sings a special song. Personally, I prefer to say "Amen." I feel I bring more glory to God by a hearty "amen," just as I would rather have people say "amen" after I pray or preach than to clap. I am aware of Psalm 47:1, "O clap your hands, all ye people; shout unto God with the voice of triumph." So, whatever our convictions are concerning these matters, may our motive be that we bring glory to God and not ourselves.

On the Judgment Day, it will not be how many gifts we were blessed with while living on this planet, but our love exhibited to our Lord and fellow men in performing the smallest to the greatest of tasks. We must remember, God is more interested in what we are than what we do. He is more concerned about our motivations than our performance.

The title of this book is *A Cup of Cold Water*. Remember, Jesus said we would not lose our reward, but let us not allow rewards to motivate us in doing good works, but love.

One of the surprises and shocks on the Day of Judgment may well be when the rewards are passed out. There will no doubt be some timid, quiet hardworking people laboring behind the scenes with little or no recognition during their probation on earth, but highly recognized in heaven. At the same time, the reverse will take place. Our Lord and Savior Jesus Christ says, "But many that are first shall be last; and the last shall be first" (St. Matthew 19:30).

As we think of small deeds with eternal significance, let us pray that God will lead us to some small deed we are capable of performing. May we not procrastinate by failing to act.

As I close this writing, I well remember the privilege I had a few years ago of bringing joy to a little girl. I was walking down the street of a city in West Virginia, when I found this little girl stranded. The chain that propelled her bicycle had slipped off and she needed help. It was not a "cup of cold water" I provided, but to me it was about as easy as giving her water. But to this youngster, it solved her problem.

These small deeds not only bring joy to the recipient, but to the donor as well. We are not saved by our good works, but by the mercy and grace of God. "For by grace are ye saved through faith; and that not of yourselves: it is the gift of God: Not of works, lest any man should boast" Ephesians 2:8-9). By the same token, we cannot remain saved without good works. "This is a faithful saying, and these things I will that thou affirm constantly, that they which have believed in God might be careful to maintain good works. These things are good and profitable unto men" (Titus 3:8). There is no contradiction in these scriptures. It has been likened to the two oars used in propelling a boat. One must use both in order to reach the destination. Otherwise, the boat would go in circles if only one oar was used.

Once we are saved and filled with the Holy Spirit, we will find that our good deeds, however small, will become a good faith tonic. In James 2:20-22, we read, "But wilt thou know, O vain man, that faith without works is dead? Was not Abraham our father justified by works, when he had offered Isaac his son upon the altar? Seest thou how faith wrought with his works, and by works was faith made perfect?"

There is no better way to conclude this book than by remembering and putting into practice the words of our blessed Lord and Savior Jesus Christ: "And whosoever shall give to drink unto one of these little ones a cup of cold water only in the name of a disciple, verily I say unto you, he shall in no wise lose his reward" (St. Matthew 10:42).